Fortune Cookie

Oracle Poetry

By Janine Palmer (Silver Moon) CHT
An Owl Feather Series

Other books by Janine Palmer

MAIN BOOKS: (First Series)

Divine Heretic – Standing Holy
Divine Heretic – In Christ Consciousness
Divine Heretic – Sacred Scribe
Divine Heretic – Mystical Fire
Divine Heretic – Alchemist
Divine Heretic – Hierophant
Divine Heretic – Hidden Keys
Divine Heretic – Wordsmith
Divine Heretic – Song of the Seraphim
Divine Heretic – Anima Mundi
Divine Heretic – Echo of Thunder
Divine Heretic – Sword of Truth
Divine Heretic – Flaming Sword
Divine Heretic – Compassionate Non-Conformist
Divine Heretic – Sacred Smoke Signals
Divine Heretic – Arrows of Light
Divine Heretic – The Edge of Inner Truth

JP SILVER MOON SERIES: (Second Series)

Magic Quill, Sacred Sword
Fire & Thunder of the Bard
Mystical Whispers of the Soul
Mystical Whispers of the Scribe

Quicksilver Ink
Owl Feather, Sacred Scribe
Recalling the Mystery, Goddess of Arc
On Winged Destrier
Points of the Queen's Crown
Whispers of the Woods
Soul Speak, Mystical Heart
Extracting Wisdom from Experience
By the Light of the Silver Moon
Divine Illumination
Spiritual Alchemy
Lady of Fire
On Ravens' Wings
Enchanted Perspectives
Shields & Swords of Light
From Mystic Realms
Winged Revelation
Mystical Whispers of the Heart
Mystical Whispers of Wisdom
Cloaked Mystery & Swords of Truth
Sacred Temple
Twinkling of Twilight
Swords & Shields of Light
From Mystic Realms
Shadow Dance
Glimpses of Soul
Journal Entries from the Dragon Path
The Midnight Moon

From the Angels of Avalon
Once a Knight
Through the Mists & Shadows
Ink of Angelic Fire
Sacred Dialogue
Bardic Fire
Smoke Signals from Sacred Fire
Arrow Flights
Forged in Sacred Flame
Through Mystical Grace
A Priestess and a Poet Scribe
Poetic Ripples
Beautiful Reflections in Tarnished Mirrors
A Gypsy, a Knight, and a Philosopher
Mystical Journeys & Sacred Travelers
Mystical Muse
Pirate Ships & Shakespeare's Lips
Little Voices Carried on the Wind
Love Notes to Self
Pirate Ships & Shakespeare's Lips
Mystical Keys of the Soul
Oak Leaves & Acorns
Grails of Silver & Gold
Foxes & Flowers
Poet's Treasures
Bard's Treasures
Poetry from the Ashes Reborn
Glimpses of Mystical Prayers

Poetic Pinpoints of Light
Mystical Keys of the Soul
Divine Messages & Sacred Seeds
From the Ashes of Heretic Fire
Notes from Sacred Realms
Thoughts Infused with Love
A Cottage in the Heart
The Castle of the Heart
Whispers from Sacred Realms
From Bardic Wisdom Keepers

OWL FEATHER SERIES: (Third Series)

Gatekeepers of Sacred Temples
Remembering Forgotten Worthiness
Reflections of Perceptions
Weaving Beauty with Gratitude
This Book
Poetic Ministrations
Treasure Boxes & Tea Parties
Reflections of Worthiness
Mystical Ink
Perspectives, Paradigms & Possibilities
Gypsy Moon Boom
Mystical Chit Chat
Kingdoms Within

GENRE SPECIFIC BOOKS:
(Material Pulled from Main Books)

Energy Healing Wisdom
Spiritual Healing Wisdom
Divine Healing Wisdom
Rising Above Dogma
For Romance
Heart Speak
Romantic Reflections
Book of Worthiness
Apocalypse of Worthiness
Scriptures of Worthiness
Providence of Worthiness
Shamanic Energy Medicine
Sacred Shamanic Whispers
Shamanic Poetic Points of Light
Shamanic Healing Wisdom
Poetic Fire
Forged in Poetic Fire
Poetic Fire of the Soul

GENRE SPECIFIC BOOKS:
(Material pulled from the JP Silver Moon
Series and Owl Feather Series)

Sometimes, Always, Never
Sometimes, Then and Now

Souvenirs of the Soul
Bardic Passion Ignited
Poetic Flame Ignited
Forged in Poetic Flame
Pulse Point Poetry

Dedication

This book is dedicated to my family with deep love and to all the people who inspired me to write and to all poets and writers. The poetry contained herein is an acknowledgement to the healing powers of writing.

Writing about the importance of processing and releasing emotions becomes artistic expression. Energy needs to flow. These tales are about releasing those blocks. Trust the process of unfolding and spiritual evolvement.

Blessings, love, and light.

Janine Palmer (Silver Moon) CHT

Acknowledgment of Gratitude

I am grateful for the blessings along my path, even the ones disguised as piles of shite. We learn from everything and everyone.

I am thankful for friends and guides and for so many amazing things learned and for the energy healing modalities I've learned, including and especially shamanic training, which helped to remember things, ancient things, I had forgotten.

I am thankful of emotional and spiritual healing which is an ongoing process. I am thankful for the opportunity to be of service and to help others when and if I can, when and if they ask for it.

I am thankful for such beautiful wisdom regained. I'm thankful for the inspiration for the writing and for how I am guided, known, or unknown. I am thankful to be able to incorporate healing messages into the poems and messages.

I am thankful for what I've learned from spiritual teachers and biblical scholars and that I have always enjoyed reading which has opened me to so much knowledge and wisdom. I am grateful to all those who believed in me.

I want to say thank you to all the friends and family who have graciously supported me, taught me, and redirected me. So many blessings.

Janine Palmer (Silver Moon) CHT

Forward

This little book reflects glimpses of experience and the wisdom gained from them. It reflects wounds, and the effects of the wounded who wound. It speaks of energy healing and forgiveness. It speaks of spiritual alchemy and the ascension of the spirit and the soul. It speaks of opening the door of the heart to love.

It speaks of battle scars and shedding skins and shells. It speaks of sacred temples and the fire of transformation. It speaks of rising above and moving beyond judgment, the spiraling, higher path to freedom through love and healing and releasing what does not serve. It speaks of the power of forgiveness. It speaks of things mystical and sacred. It speaks of magic.

It speaks of angels and dragons and divine love. It speaks of mirrors, treasures, keys and the mystical. It speaks of shadow and perspectives. It speaks of spirit, heart, soul, and light. It speaks of deeper truth beyond belief and hidden keys. It basically shares the depth of love revealed by life experiences.

Introduction

What is shared in my writings often comes from wisdom gained through experiences, sometimes very grueling experiences. What is shared is also tools and knowledge gained from many healing modalities and certifications as well as much study of religions, religious scholars, and spiritual teachers.

My work is for the purpose of reminding people to their worthiness and rising above judgement as far as condemnation of others due to lack of compassion or understanding.

These little stories offer information about healing self and stepping away from or letting go of toxic energies. Everyone interprets them differently. What I speak of comes from being shattered. Some of what I write comes from the parts of me which survived and endeavored to tell the tales and share what I learned.

Many of us do what we feel called to do for the collective, for the greater good...whatever our perception of that is. There are many

unhealed wounds in this world, in people, in the earth, and in animals.
There are unhealed wounds in ancestral lines. These unattended wounds often cause people to go out and create more wounds.

We can do the work if we feel called to. The writing in this (and these) books are for those who have taken a step out on the path and are already moving out of stagnation and programming, or those who are ready to.

JP Silver Moon (CHT)

Contents

Sacred Temple

Outspoken is a language she speaks fluently
depending on inspiration or necessity.

Sacred Temple

We might learn something we wish we didn't
know, and we might have to unlearn
something that doesn't need to be used to
control us through programs of guilt, shame,
and fear. We will be drawn to our own ways
to be loving and proactive in a collective
way.

Sacred Temple

I am my own fortress and my own temple
complete with secret entrance and escape
route. The map to navigate the illusion is
updated as needed.

Sacred Temple

A temple so holy,
In a forgotten space,
Adjusting the light,
Returning to grace.

Making mistakes,
Known or unknown,
But still loving ourselves,
While we work to atone.

Sacred Temple

So often we might feel confident in our
decisions and our actions, but something
might happen to make us question what we
did or didn't do.

Reflection is part of our learning process.

Sacred Temple

A crackling fire,
An ancient book,
The ones they kept,
The ones they took.

Modern day gospels,
Of evolving good news,
As always forthcoming,
Understood by the few.

Sacred Temple

Antidote or elixir,
To the poison of untruth,
The ways which we must heal,
From what proved to be uncouth.

Stepping out of the matrix,
Out of dogma's box,
Powerful in our innate light,
Shattering the locks.

Sacred Temple

Glimpses of Soul

Was she distant or was she disconnected
from levels of suffering that were like
whirlpools trying to suck her in?

Maybe she just preferred to cultivate peace
and love. Maybe she preferred perspectives
with zoom lenses.

Glimpses of Soul

Does the trauma create detachment?
Obscuring destiny or fate?
An arena where we choose,
Between the energy of love or hate.

Glimpses of Soul

There is peace to be found in the
caves my ancestors inhabited.

Glimpses of Soul

Yes, she was kind,
But she could also be fierce,
Her heart she kept hidden,
So it would not be pierced.

None of Cupid's darts,
Were invited her way,
Because a love lived within her,
No fairy tale could slay.

Glimpses of Soul

She was drawn to enchantment,
Now and before,
Veiled curiosity,
Knocked at her door.

Dragging a sword,
Wrapped in dark lace,
And a telltale smile,
Animating her face.

Glimpses of Soul

How dark is the tunnel?
On our way home?
What treasures are buried?
Wherever we roam?

What stories are written?
Interpreted or perceived?
To what truth or what falsehood,
Do we continue to cleave?

Glimpses of Soul

From types of poison,
The antidote might come,
And from the opposite,
Some of us run.

Truth tells stories,
But who might hear?
Does it come from love?
Or does it come from fear?

Glimpses of Soul

Mystical & Sacred

From Myth or Mystery

What inspires a being to 'awaken'?
From what might be considered a dream?
When do we begin to discover,
That things aren't what they seem?

How much is twisted by religious programming?
Through the energy of fear?
How much love is woven in,
Through what we do or do not hear?

Who might pass along important knowledge?
And how much judgment might interfere?
How do we realize higher purpose?
And the reasons we are here?

What ripples out from myth or mystery?
And how does or doesn't it apply?
To rediscovering the sacred truths,
Which exist in you and I?

What shackles, chains, or fraying ropes,
Might we now release?
To expel now from our sacred space,
The energy of the thief?

What traumas do we carry?
Even if unknown?
When do we begin to transmute the wounds?
And what must we atone?

What parts of us are trying to speak?
And do we really hear?
Clearer becomes the perspective,
When we rise above false fear.

When it's not about monsters outside of ourselves,
No matter what labels we use,
When we step back into our sovereignty,
By our free will choice, we choose.

Beware of so many distractions,
Which might try to pull you in,
To keep you fighting and draining your energy,
Is ignorance the sin?

So many now are rising,
Out of unnecessary prisons cells,
Discovering they hold the keys,
As light shines into hell.

Janine Palmer (Silver Moon)

Mystical & Sacred

Sword and hammer, axe, and bow,
Simple truths we already know,
Disengaging from battles, where darkness feeds,
To concentrate on more wholesome needs.

Mystical & Sacred

He said, "I have no words. Your voice like a
sweet melody, is a whisper of sweetness. But
who is your soul? I find everything magical
in what you say, bloody poetic. Every
syllable has a melody. Who did you write it
to or for?

I will listen over and over again. Your soul is
wonderful. I am fascinated by it. I have so
much to learn from your words. It can be
upsetting. Real poems are harsh."

Mystical & Sacred

Iron and wood,
The castle door,
What we gather,
From the threshing floor.

Angels among us,
Seen or not,
And our everlasting worthiness,
Most of us forgot.

Mystical & Sacred

Shingles of slate,
On a cottage of old,
The books they refer to,
Of what was foretold.

Through different decisions,
Beyond dogma's hold,
Some became alchemists,
Of spiritual gold.

Mystical & Sacred

Libraries of liberation,
Awaken in the soul's domain,
And once you exercise your sovereignty,
Your true power you regain.

Mystical & Sacred

Divine Wisdom

Hidden Thieves

Resentment is not my master,
Judgement is not my battlefield,
Illusion is a trickster,
But my truth it shall not steal.

Fundamentalism is a bully,
The leader of an egoic gang,
And there are those who refuse to engage,
In self-superior slang.

Like a pack of wolves so hungry,
On gossip they like to feed,
Seemingly oblivious or uncaring,
About whom they cause to bleed.

Nefarious and underhanded,
Childish behavior of those full grown,
What their thoughts and actions reveal,
And for what they must atone.

A parliament of puppets,
Programmed to the hilt,
Not taking responsibility,
For burning bridges, the humble built.

Feeling justified in thoughts and actions,
Obedient to false belief,
Unkind to fellow humans,
Beware the hidden thief.

Spirit Silver Moon

Divine Wisdom

Epiphany

We go through certain experiences,
To which we respond or react,
Depending on our perspectives,
And the fullness or lack of facts.

We might react to what something appears to be,
Which might not be entirely true,
And the emotions we feel because of it,
Might block love from coming through.

We might feel somewhat resentful,
But hopefully we can learn to let it go,
It might branch off something unrecognized,
Which might just dim our glow.

People would tell me they sensed a sadness in me,
And I wondered from whence it came,
It took years for me to realize,
What hidden emotions were to blame.

I'd felt the effects of types of betrayal,
From different people in my life,
Things they did or didn't do,
Which felt like a cut from a knife.

Unknowingly holding onto emotion,
Not realizing it was there,
So-called betrayal, sadness, and resentment,
Such a diabolical snare.

That which we don't see in ourselves,
Even though we're working to heal,
Until we go deeper into it and there's an epiphany,
The layers we all must peel.

One word stood out while I was reading,
Then somehow, I finally knew,
The energy or emotion I'd been carrying,
How wonderful when wisdom shines through.

What I'd been unknowingly carrying,
Was drawing in more of the same,
Experiences meant to show me something,
That I didn't realize I needed to tame.

Energy reflecting energy,
In ways we might not yet see,
Stumbling blocks of emotion,
That keep us temporarily unfree.

Spirit Silver Moon

Divine Wisdom

Flashes

A light bulb moment when it struck me,
What emotions had been holding me back,
Imprisoned in stagnation,
Inviting me to take my power back.

To let it go, to move and flow,
To replace it with something higher,
Not holding anything against another,
So balance and healing can transpire.

A sudden shift in my energy,
When mind and heart connected due to one word,
And that which has been trying to speak to me,
Could finally be heard.

Spirit Silver Moon

Divine Wisdom

Battle scenes,
Lived and died,
War and peace,
However tried.

Ego's drama,
Colored bright,
Until love shall win,
With all our might.

Divine Wisdom

Historical fancy,
Of memories past,
The light that still lingers,
The love that will last.

So much forgotten,
While creating the new,
As whispers of love,
Always flow through.

Divine Wisdom

Energy Healing

When abominable behavior inspires someone
to stand in their power and speak
inconvenient truth, there might be backlash
when people don't like what's being reflected
to them or what they don't want to face.

It seems easier to avoid taking responsibility
and to blame or find fault with others. Don't
allow dysfunction to be dumped on you that
isn't yours. Self-honesty is something not
everyone is comfortable with. Honor yourself
and others whenever possible. Integrity is a
superpower.

Energy Healing

The venom of hatred is never stronger,
Than love which is the cure,
There must come a pivotal point,
When something dark is not the lure.

Energy Healing

It's upsetting when relationships fall apart
due to jealousy, people talking unkindly
behind your back. Egoic fuckery which pours
out of wounded beings.

We might say it or write it in such a raw,
truthful, intense way that it might make us
laugh very loudly. It's part of the healing
process.

Energy Healing

We might learn the hard way that those who
cloak themselves in victim energy don't
make the best friends or partners.

Energy Healing

A ghost from the past,
That beloved voice,
The soul recognition,
The heart's precious choice.

Energy Healing

The emotions she released were merely ghost
stories that got stuck behind closed or
forgotten doors.

Energy Healing

Once upon a different time,
Similar lessons did occur,
And until our choices change,
They'll still be what they were.

Energy Healing

Fire of Transformation

Speaking truth, however subtly or
passionately to those not ready to face it, can
be dangerous. This is when vampires might
come out to feed.

Fire of Transformation

Inspiration knocks on many doors,
Revealing mysteries to explore,
Wiser now than I was before,
And love shall lead, forevermore.

Fire of Transformation

Most people want a connection. They crave
it. They don't want a competition. But some
thrive off competition. It's important to be
aware of what we are aligning with.

Fire of Transformation

Many people are gifted and use their gifts for
good or helpful purposes, to be of service
through kindness and compassion.

Some people misuse their gifts to harm others
which is a very unpleasant and destructive
energy.

We might have to choose who or what
energy is or isn't welcome or allowed in our
space.

Fire of Transformation

A campfire at the mouth of a cave,
As prayers go up with the smoke,
As we release the pain from emotion,
And illusion dissipates, making room for
hope.

Fire of Transformation

Come along on this journey,
So we may recall,
A love so important,
Nothing can forestall.

Fire of Transformation

The glowing embers,
The glistening tears,
Lessons and treasures,
Through earthly years.

An opening heart,
A benevolent smile,
A flicker of romance,
Designed to beguile.

Fire of Transformation

Spiritual Alchemy

Battlefields of Duality and Polarity

So much is connected to our responses to those we speak to, or what we study, or how deeply we study…to what awakens in us. Also, depending on our experiences and our reactions to what goes on around us or to what it appears to be. We might notice ongoing battles which we give our energy and attention to or whereby it is taken from us.

Some might speak of ongoing angelic wars which are connected to and affect humanity as we navigate this realm of amnesia. This realm of duality and polarity. Where we observe or experience things which have opposing sides. Unless and until we have experienced something opposite of what we believe, we might be lacking knowledge.

To lack knowledge from firsthand experience might create an imbalance. It might create or sustain a belief which might make us feel justified in our limited perspectives, but it might lack compassion due to what is still unknown. We might feel compelled or coerced to take sides against something or someone. It might be egoic in nature and we might not realize it.

It might be political, religious, or even a debilitating battle between masculine and feminine. It might be distracting us from existing in a sovereign state and it might distract us from doing our own healing. We might be too busy trying to blame someone or something else that either has power over us or that we unknowingly give our power to.

We might gather wisdom and decide through our own free agency to detach or disentangle ourselves from certain belief systems which pit us against one another. Something which grows stronger from our suffering, anger, or unforgiveness. When we step out of the battlefields of belief, we might level up to a more elevated state of our own innate 'power'.

When we consciously decide what we are going to give our energy to and what we are not going to give our energy to, then we are more in control of ourselves than outside sources. It might also behoove us to remember that not everything is as it seems. There is so much illusion and so much missing or hidden knowledge which skews our perspectives.

We are always invited to choose or create something more peaceful, but in order to do that we might need to cut invisible puppet strings.

So much is affected or created by our thoughts, many of which aren't even true. Much of the time we might be too much in our minds, being tortured by false thoughts, false beliefs, and programming. Do we forget to consult the heart?

Being programmed or conditioned might come from ingrained belief systems, whether religious, political, or cultural. Also, from that which is passed down through families from generations of suffering. Some people begin to realize that it doesn't serve them and choose to break away from those ties that bind and that is powerful.

Some might think they are being loyal to something they feel they shouldn't question. There are many types of slavery which aren't recognized as such. We are here to learn to love one another, but so many paradigms create separation or the illusion of it and so much of it works through the ego.

Discovering, opening to, and sharing love and compassion ripples out to and from something far bigger than ourselves.

Resentment, anger, self-righteousness and unforgiveness can be like invisible shackles to a self-made hell.

We have the power to make different choices, to unlearn and to discover inner truth. We have the keys to our kingdoms, but we might have to search for them through the process of letting go of the lies of unworthiness and remembering the beauty of our divinity and the love from whence we came.

Something way beyond the mistranslations or misuse or incompleteness of the scriptures people allow to rule them which were only meant to guide them. That which was taken too literally, skewed, or hijacked from its original purpose or intention.

Stories have been passed down, myths, metaphors, and parables from which to extract spiritual teachings. Things that have been twisted and altered and unless one endeavors to truly study, they might remain grossly unaware of this. Minds closed in belief can be like prison cells of stagnation. Our lives are great opportunities for many things, but fear too often inhibits that.

There is so much to learn and so much to unlearn.
There is so much love to share and so many in need of
it. Finding fault through limited perspectives to
bolster ego is thorny pathway to a dark place. Love is
the light that liberates.

JP Silver Moon

Spiritual Alchemy

It's okay to create an atmosphere of beauty
with what you perceive to be beautiful or
artistic. It's okay to appreciate things of
character which others might not recognize
as meaningful. It's not their path or their
canvas.

We are all on healing journeys and we work
on letting go but we still have hobbies and
passions it's okay to embrace, honor and
celebrate what we find beautiful or
inspirational.

Spiritual Alchemy

Love so magnificent,
It doesn't die, it's reborn,
Lifetime through lifetime,
Mending what's torn.

A window, a doorway,
A poem so profound,
And in its great whirlpool,
No one can drown.

Spiritual Alchemy

Worthiness & Wings

Sometimes you must let go of the shame you
carry from the false judgment of others,
because it simply isn't yours to carry.

It's connected to programs and the thought
forms which feed them. Free yourself
through higher perspectives.

Worthiness & Wings

People might function in a type of fantasy or
maybe it's simply their truth. Their
interpretation of what's real or illusionary.

Many poetic writers don't write so much
fantasy as they do feelings. Maybe my
romantic poems are wishes or glimpses of
memories.

For myself, most of my writing is my
interpretation of God's work or how I might
be of service in that way.

Worthiness & Wings

Threads once woven might come undone,
As we come to know the holy one,
As we come to remember that divinity exists,
Through the ages of love, we've dared to
kiss.

Worthiness & Wings

She said, "There are ways in which I conduct
myself where I know I am fair, thoughtful,
and compassionate. I know I can be very
careful and tactful with my tone and my
choice of words. I do what I feel is right.

Other times I might lose my patience, or I
might be triggered where my tone is more
intense, or my manner and words are more
direct. Sometimes I get upset and raise my
voice due to anger or emotion. I might cry.

It might also be a boundary or a warning that
I won't tolerate any more of what might be
trying to draw me in to a lower vibrational
energy. People might feel uncomfortable
with it, and I might feel embarrassed later.

However, sometimes people create or
contribute to the situation which they might
not take responsibility for and just blame
someone else for what they don't know how
to face in themselves. That which is
unrecognized. The battleground.

Worthiness & Wings

Some people move to the beat of their own drum. They might not comply exactly with certain control systems, but they are still honest people.

Worthiness & Wings

The sadness has lifted,
It's moving away,
Acknowledged and released,
Not invited to stay.

Clearing the temple,
Of unnecessary debris,
Emotions once stuck,
That do not serve me.

Worthiness & Wings

She embraced the world,
Only to find,
It was caught in a web,
Of unnecessary crime.

Worthiness & Wings

Blessed Be Our Magic

Cottage Flowers

An English cottage,
With stories to tell,
Where history lingers,
And mysteries dwell.

Tragedies and treasures,
Where love overcomes hate,
Where love is a greeting,
Which hangs on the gate.

Where time periods mingle,
Leaving their mark,
To inspire the imagination,
To kindle a spark.

Inspiration of the ancients,
However it speaks,
Like correspondence from an unseen
messenger,
Or a sweet elixir to drink.

Janine Palmer (Silver Moon)

Blessed Be Our Magic

Watermark

Sometimes you must look for something,
To know that it exists,
Sometimes you must communicate,
Romantically for a kiss.

Sometimes you need the right light,
For what's written to be revealed,
Sometimes our innate divinity,
Is the only thing that heals.

Janine Palmer (Silver Moon)

Blessed Be Our Magic

Shoreline

What do I see from my viewpoint?
And what might I have missed?
What flows and what is stagnant?
How do I cherish love's true bliss?

Those times when emotion changes my
voice,
Those waves coming to the shore,
Maybe that's the treasure,
To let fresh air in through the door.

The character of my being,
The wisdom or knowing which I brought in,
Stumbling through amnesia,
In chaos and peace, we swim.

A swirling of conflicting energies,
Animating my sacred space,
Ascending along the spiral,
Reintegrating grace.

Janine Palmer (Silver Moon)

Blessed Be Our Magic

It's powerful when we realize which
emotions we've been holding onto which
might create more of the same experiences.

When we acknowledge them and there's a
shift because we are ready to let them go. To
make room for more love which we give to
ourselves.

Blessed Be Our Magic

Shackles disintegrate,
As my thoughts change,
When programs don't rule,
From realms deranged.

Voices which whisper,
For me to learn,
What needs to shift,
What needs to burn.

Blessed Be Our Magic

A noticeable chill,
Felt in the air,
As Autumn comes,
Into my lair.

A change in vibration,
A cozy atmosphere,
As so many rejoice,
This time of year.

Blessed Be Our Magic

A deepening connection,
A glimpse of romance,
In illusion's realm,
Doesn't stand a chance.

A rare occurrence,
But magical still,
When honor and integrity,
Coexist through free will.

Blessed Be Our Magic

Deeper Truth

He said, "You might ask me, 'Why do you love me?' I would answer, 'Through your words. There is a complexity. Because when I talk to you, this is what we write back and forth, I am happy. Because I believe in your image and your words. Because I love everything about you.

I am an explicit person. I say what I see and respond to what I read. Bottom line is I love you too much. I need someone like you. My despair is not being with you. You don't know how many thoughts I have for you, like walking with you in the woods and talking about souls."

She said, "There is something in or about the words in the writings that speak to you on a deep level. We are drawn to things we recognize on some level even if we don't know exactly what it is or why."

He said, "I feel you inside me. I don't know how to explain, but there is a strange force inside me that says, 'Find her.'"

Deeper Truth

A candle flickering in an ancient cave,
Where I might go to conquer the knave,
Where trapped emotion can be released,
For peace to replace the feeling of grief.

Deeper Truth

I might be a storyteller,
Where emotions speak through ink,
My own healing might be an elixir,
That only I can drink.

Deeper Truth

Righteousness shouldn't be ruthless,
But experiences reveal many masks,
And if you want to learn more,
You only need to ask.

(Inquire within…)

Deeper Truth

A frozen heartbeat,
No, it's not,
It's just a glimpse of love,
The world forgot.

Deeper Truth

There are ghosts of memories and
emotions waiting to speak through
her ink.

Deeper Truth

It's up to us on an individual level to remain
as steadfastly aware as possible in these times
of upheaval and change. That probably
includes being open to alternative
perspectives.

There are twisted, imbalanced thoughts,
programming and actions happening all over
the globe. There are entities which are
making fuckery fashionable.

We all have an inner compass, but we might
have to recognize and step out of the
propaganda. We might need to look deeper,
beyond the fiction, to be able to recognize
truth and honor it in our own way.

Deeper Truth

Mirror, Mirror

He said, "I showed my friend some of your
poems. She said you're good for me. I love
your light and what you convey in your
heartfelt words. You conquered the dark and
showed me how."

Mirror, Mirror

Perception might translate a story,
Which may or may not be true,
As we move through transformation,
Back to the love of me and you.

Mirror, Mirror

Many have been my adventures,
And the treasure I chose to collect,
My art may or may not be visible,
Through how I choose to reflect.

Mirror, Mirror

A reflection brilliant,
Within his eyes,
And words with the power,
To penetrate disguise.

Mirror, Mirror

Her friend said, "Did you know that you have
connections with angels? Every time I see
your picture you are glowing.

Mirror, Mirror

He said, "I took the liberty of showing your
media profile to a friend of mine. He told me,
'My God she is a goddess.' I replied, yes, she
is, but she is beyond this world."

She said, "I find it interesting how you see
me which is probably different than I see
myself."

Mirror, Mirror

He said, "I don't love easily. I'm not a
playboy, but I need to see soul. I'm a simple,
common man, perhaps trivial. But to give my
heart, I need to see soul in a woman. It
doesn't matter if you're a Madonna or a
model or a famous woman. I have to feel
your soul to be in love with you.

I can feel your soul."

Mirror, Mirror

Battle Scars & Shedding Skins

Sometimes you might try to help someone,
but you can't. It's their issue to acknowledge,
address and 'fix'. Interference might be like
entering a lion's den. The lion of ego. We
might be interfering with an important,
possibly karmic, learning experience.

Battle Scars & Shedding Skins

A Wretched Den of Scum & Villainy

Is 'wretched' a perspective?
Or a suffering state of mind?
Is it a vibration?
Reflecting peace, we can't yet find?

When crime becomes 'accepted',
And fighting it isn't allowed,
It's a time when we are witnessing,
The dark behind the shroud.

The imbalance and the fuckery,
Of extremism making waves,
A wretched den of scum and villainy,
Of the trickster and the knave.

Title from a line of dialogue in 'Star Wars'

Battle Scars and Shedding Skins

Some people have an inner battle going on
which they project onto another. Sometimes
we're not aware of how our energy ripples
out or how harmful it can be.

Battle Scars & Shedding Skins

I tripped over something rancid,
Contaminating my path,
I might have stumbled and skinned my knees,
But I still know how to laugh.

Battle Scars & Shedding Skins

Buyer Beware

This world of greed and suffering,
Systems forcing people to pay,
To exist in a plane of duality,
Where gluttonous corporations and people try to seize
the day.

Insurance companies selling required policies,
Which they try to slither out of having to pay,
And something more nefarious is backing them,
Contributing to the decay.

Chemical peddlers of 'medicines',
Who ignore other methods to heal,
Keeping people in ignorance,
So their money they can steal.

Greed the worship of money, their god,
And false power, a destructive force,
Making slaves of people unapologetically,
But some make different choices, of course.

Medical industries trying to control a market,
In certain unethical ways,
But some people realize they have other options,
And that's when they exit the maze.

Now is a time to be careful,
It's a time to become and remain aware,
Not everything is as it seems,
As usual, buyer beware.

Inflation and unaffordable housing,
Corrupt governments and dictators abound,
We've forgotten how to take our sovereignty back,
Or that hope can always be found.

Finding ways to make ends meet,
And infusing love into everything,
Letting go of ideologies,
Embracing inspiration when it sings.

The world as we knew it is changing,
And in certain ways it must,
But sometimes it seems we're being swept along,
In impersonal robotic waves of disgust.

We are here for experience,
Not to be outdone by man-made machines,
We are the ones, after all,
Who still know how to dream.

Spirit Silver Moon

Battle Scars & Shedding Skins

Sometimes what we say or write is for the purpose of
looking deeper and for thinking or feeling more.

The process of processing and moving energy.

Battle Scars & Shedding Skins

Treasure & Keys

We might learn something we wish we didn't
know, and we might have to unlearn
something that doesn't need to be used to
control us through programs of guilt, shame,
and fear.

We will be drawn to our own ways to be
loving and productive in a collective way.

Treasure & Keys

Ambience is my inspiration,
And love that dares to speak,
And how it feels in my heart and soul,
Whether I laugh or weep.

Treasure & Keys

Keys to locks on her heart's door,
Lost or found on the threshing floor,
Words can be keys as we might know,
Which can melt the ice and kindle the glow.

Treasure & Keys

There are keys still within me,
Which might remain unseen,
Guarding pockets of knowledge,
Which are not part of the dream.

Treasure & Keys

The silence in what is spoken,
And what a simple glance might speak,
The knowing feeling of the soul,
An open heart might greet.

Treasure & Keys

She said, "Do you dare to look deep within
yourself to find the treasures of truth and
beauty and allow them to speak?"

Treasure & Keys

A shimmering energy,
Most can't see,
As long as it's moving,
It represents 'free'.

Stagnation is prison,
Like a stifled voice,
Like stuck emotion,
And forgotten choice.

Treasure & Keys

Suffering & Shadow

Some people don't want solutions to their
dramas and battles because something in
them feeds off it.

Suffering & Shadow

Sometimes trying to be helpful, say at work,
to find solutions between people engaged in
ego battles, might cause someone to perceive
you as 'the enemy'. Someone to blame,
another target for unresolved resentment. Not
a good fit, which might also translate to, not
of the same vibration.

I can create clashes. Different viewpoints
from different perceptions. Perspectives can
be skewed or tainted by belief, programming,
walls, and the wounds we subconsciously try
to protect. Sometimes we are mirrors and
people don't like what we reflect to them so
we might be perceived as a nemesis.

It has much to do with the presence or
absence of light and what is or isn't yet seen
or known. Unresolved issues and
unprocessed emotions block light and the
flow of energy. It requires courage to face
what was or is painful. Anger and resentment
point to something deeper, wanting to be
heard. There are different ways in which we
must learn to speak.

Suffering & Shadow

He seems to choose to be a victim,
Even if unconsciously so,
Which makes him the type of person,
It's almost impossible to know.

Suffering & Shadow

After a triggered or heated dialogue about the politics or corruption of the world, she said to her friend, "If you could put aside your hatred for a few minutes, maybe meditate on that. Maybe call in your angels and guides and ask them to show you something you need to be more aware of.

Ask, 'What am I missing? What do I need to see? What do I need to be open enough to see or to realize to shift out of hatred?' What might that be? Not everybody is willing to do that work. That's shadow work. So, if you weren't hating on somebody, who would you be? If you weren't hating on somebody, where would you be in your life?

If you could step out of the hatred for a minute, what might you see that you missed? What might you not be seeing? There are things that people refuse to see and its right out there in the open if you look."

Suffering & Shadow

It's not that one side is any better than the
other or any more righteous than the other.
They do have different agendas. There might
be 'good' things in those agendas or there
might be shady things in those agendas.

People might see it, or they might not see it.
That might be true that might not be true. I'm
pretty sure there's some truth in there. So, we
must determine what that truth is for
ourselves and hopefully, we can do it without
hatred.

There are good things that come from certain
administrations or organizations. Because it's
not just the puppets that some people hate,
it's the people behind them who are
temporarily running the show. Who the hell
are they and what are they up to? Oh, that's
just a 'conspiracy!' Is it though? Is it really?

Suffering & Shadow

Is it a tunnel or is it a cave?
Is it a minister or is it a knave?
Is it a swamp or a healing spring?
Is belief a falsehood to which we cling?

Suffering & Shadow

Gaslighting on an epic level is playing out on
the world stage. Defending sides through
anger and hatred won't change it.

Only a change in perspective and choice can
make a difference now. Fare thee well and
peace be with you.

Suffering & Shadow

Whispers from the Heart

So often we might feel confident in our
decisions and our actions, but something
might happen to make us question what we
did or didn't do and why.

Reflection is part of the learning process. It's
part of the healing process. It's part of the
process of making peace and finding
different, valid perspectives.

It's when we discover that things aren't
exactly what we thought they were, and we
become wiser. Sifting through the chaff.

Whispers from the Heart

He said, "I can't find the right words for you,
but I can tell you my soul loves you. I have a
lot of flaws but I'm honest and I'm not afraid
to say I love you. I am fascinated by your
being, your beauty, your soul, etc."

Whispers from the Heart

She said, "I have always been a person who
loves romance and romantic things.

And those things have not been a part of my
life for a long time, except for what comes
out in my writing periodically.

It lives in me whether inspired or uninspired.

I think I went from being emotional to
detached. Too much protection from the
wounds of the wounded."

Whispers from the Heart

He said, "The greatest work of emotion in this world is love. There is nothing beyond this in the world."

She said, "For me, it seems to be stuck, buried, or hidden. The love is always there, and it shines through in different ways. What is absent is a direct connection of giving and receiving and expressing that love in balance."

He said, "There are no obstacles, it's a thin line of well-being. It's beautiful to be loved, reciprocation. Tell me what is more important in this wrong world than love. Nothing. Loving your neighbor is the most beautiful thing in this world."

She said, "Yes, it's all true. It doesn't mean we experience it continually at all times."

He said, "Poetry springs from love."

She said, "Yes, or from pain and suffering. That buried love trying to blossom again."

He said, "Everything was born for this."

She said, "Much of it is an illusion."

He said, "Yes, love brings suffering."

She said, "Because we hope or think it's something different than what it is."

He said, "But it is an example that we live."

She said, "It seems like the way it touches people deeply is something that flickers in an out of our existence or awareness. An example that we try to live even though we are often fooled and confused by illusionary things."

Whispers from the Heart

Ashes & Ink

It was the end of her exile,
The separation, however made,
Consciously or unconsciously,
The glimmer of the blade.

On the edge of unknowing,
As realization unfolds upon a darkened path,
Trying to bring back the parts of her that left,
When the weight of trauma pushed her back.

She disconnected from her emotions,
Then went on a quest to find,
Ways in which to remember herself,
Cutting ties that should not bind.

What was reflected back to her,
Was something she didn't understand,
She reached out in the darkness,
Not knowing who might take her hand.

The wounded guiding the wounded,
Doing the best they can,
Until the lack of necessary integrity,
Forces one to take a stand.

Stepping onto a solitary path,
To bring oneself back into the light,
As the glow from within illuminates the map,
Out of the soul's dark night.

Inner growth through a grueling gauntlet,
A warrior is reborn,
Molded and sculpted from the hardened ash,
And mending what was torn.

Rebuilding what was broken,
Rising from what burned,
Becoming the sacred ink to write,
The next page to be turned.

Janine Palmer (Silver Moon)

Whispers from the Heart

Light through the Cracks

Revolutionary Power

The revolutions that are necessary,
To take our power back,
From entities dark and nefarious,
To move to joy from lack.

Not an orchestra of puppets,
Hypnotized by some newscast,
Not manipulated through fear,
Not tethered to the past.

Creating something more loving,
Reclaiming our sovereignty again,
From greedy and corrupt corporations,
Our subscriptions we rescind.

Not taking the illusionary bait,
Ignoring the hook, line, and sinker,
To become our own investigator,
And not a programmed under thinker.

Dysfunction swirling around us,
Sending us hither and yon,
It's time for us to recognize and claim,
The path we should be on.

The roadblocks of bureaucracy,
Interfere with our experiences here,
Trying to dishonor our free will,
Trying to bind through false belief and fear.

But we don't need to support it,
We can make another choice,
We don't need to be a victim,
To rediscover our sacred voice.

It will require our self-honesty,
And an ability to see past what's fake,
Because the inner truth we hold to firmly,
Darkness cannot take.

Spirit Silver Moon

Light through the Cracks

Exploring things of primal source,
Something magical guides, of course,
Something ancient longs to speak,
To breach the door of a forgotten keep.

Light through the Cracks

Her friend said, "Absolutely beautiful. I love
your imagery and the hope you offer, in the
dark."

She said, "In the dark?"

Her friend said, "The darkness of the
muddled confusion and lack of clarity and
lies that the constant stream of information
and propaganda brings and the division it
causes.

You have such a gift with words. I truly
appreciate that you see a way to get to the
light at the end of the tunnel. It's hard to do
sometimes."

Thank you, MW

Light through the Cracks

Blowing out the smoke and ash,
Of the destruction ignorance made,
So, love can come in to heal,
And the trauma can now fade.

Light through the Cracks

Letters written,
Stories told,
Glimpses of wisdom,
Seeds of gold.

Inspiration kindled,
From sacred fire,
As alchemy unfolds,
Through what transpires.

Light through the Cracks

Poetry as a messenger,
From the place where our souls speak,
With pen, parchment, and intention,
Through the ink we weep.

Wisdom the language we're learning,
The pearls we leave behind,
Glimpses and treasures of the mountains,
We were brave enough to climb.

Light through the Cracks

Spoken from the Soul

There might be people who want to fight
against you, but you don't have to engage in
those battles.

You can remove yourself, or sometimes
outside sources might move you or redirect
you out of that space.

It might feel like rejection, but it might be
redirection not yet recognized.

Spoken from the Soul

Sometimes we stay in situations, relationships, or workplace, where the behaviors or energies of others are challenging for us.

We stay because there are aspects of it that are good or that we enjoy. We might feel we have something to offer, and we might receive something that is good for us.

We might not realize the vibe has changed to a degree that isn't good for us. We might try to work through it or remain loyal to something, but it falls apart.

We might feel sad or confused if we were getting mixed signals, etc. It's a process to learn to go with the flow of things. It's good to reflect, to change perspective and to let go.

Hopefully we don't overthink it. Hopefully we don't hold things against ourselves or others. There are things outside of us we can't 'fix'. Working within our own energy and creating peace is something we have the power to do.

Spoken from the Soul

There are those for whom,
Money is not king,
Something much more meaningful,
Continues now to sing.

There are those who are not,
So seduced by greed,
Who aren't controlled by dark entities,
Wanting and needing to feed.

There are those who are guided,
From a more compassionate place,
Those who seem to embody,
An element of grace.

Those who care about others,
Not only just themselves,
Who reach out a helping hand,
To guide the way out of hell.

It's a time of apocalypse,
To reveal what's been hidden,
As we cleanse and we purge,
Not to do as we might be bidden.

To think for ourselves,
Not shackled by groupthink,
To you break free of slave systems,
Also known as beliefs.

To come back to our joy,
Which exists from within,
As we are never unworthy,
Beware misinterpretation of sin.

Janine Palmer (Silver Moon)

Spoken from the Soul

Obscured

Labels and supposed conspiracies,
And energies of planets and full moons,
The masks of ideologies we might wear,
Whether wise man or buffoon.

Seriously concerned or oblivious,
The battles we might choose to fight,
In the arena of the ego,
And illusions of wrong and right.

Where perspectives become battlegrounds,
And missing information might just maim,
Where rigid ideologies and closed minds,
Keep so many people stumbling and lame.

What some seem to see, and others don't,
Does not a straight line make,
We must endeavor to discover,
What is real and what it fake.

Truth might be subjective,
From experience or indoctrination,
And through our inalienable free will,
We might seek and choose liberation.

Caught like fish upon sharp hooks,
Not recognizing where danger lurks,
Especially if too busy reacting and fighting,
Because darkness got there first.

Moving emotions for clarity,
Allowing feelings to flow,
Working on our triggers,
As there is so much, we don't know.

Truth speakers have always been persecuted,
By those trying to be in control,
Have we learned nothing from the history
some are trying to erase or obscure?
They will never dim our glow.

Our ancestors suffered through ignorance,
But we can choose to learn,
As we sift the wheat from the chaff,
And let the falsehood burn.

Spirit Silver Moon

Spoken from the Soul

Bubble Gum Keep

If mystical fairy tales,
Dance in her heart,
Is she afraid,
Of cupid's dart?

Did it once sting her?
In a terrible way?
Are the sutures of wounds,
Starting to fray?

Are her windows and doors,
Open to fresh air?
Can she feel it in the dream?
The one who waits there?

Is amnesia the barrier?
Her bubble gum walls,
Does she even believe,
It will happen at all?

What changed her perspective?
She who would rather dive deep?
When she gives you her love,
It becomes yours to keep.

Janine Palmer (Silver Moon)

Beyond Belief

So many people worship the vessel of a
messenger and not so much how to apply the
wisdom the messages contain. This is how
cults are started under other names.

Beyond Belief

People will create a problem due to thoughts
and actions, feeling justified, and then feel
offended by the counter actions of others who
are trying to find solutions to the problem.

They declare a silent, vindictive war. It's a
battle in which they are they only participant
until someone pushes back with a reflective
shield and is then perceived as the enemy.

Diabolical shenanigans.

Beyond Belief

What poison lurks invisible?
But some sense something is wrong?
What lies are sold as truth?
From the stage fear rules upon.

Are we so seduced by the fear of climate change?
That we help the overlords put the shackles on?
Are we so fearful of some sickness?
That we allow our freedom to be trampled upon?

Is being controlled some kind of comfort?
When should we not conform?
How much calm resides within us?
As we weather this terrible storm.

Is the darkness an unholy master?
Whom we allow to rule?
But who are they who choose?
To exit the valley of the fool?

Are we encouraged to dislike what's true?
To battle it within ourselves?
Are we ever aware?
Of the different levels of hell?

Hell on earth through false belief,
Which some now hail as king,
Until we learn to recognize illusion,
And the suffering it brings.

Gathering information is recommended,
Whether or not it's perceived as fact,
Because at some point on this treacherous ride,
We might want to take our power back.

Spirit Silver Moon

Beyond Belief

Within the flames, we might just see,
A glimpse of something, pure and free,
And through intention, we create,
In charge of our destiny, not bound by fate.

Beyond Belief

Resurrecting beautiful friendships,
Instead of throwing them away,
Infusing them with new light,
Not letting them decay.

They are our greatest teachers,
Mirrors of ourselves now and then,
Windows and doors still opening,
Allowing blessings to come in.

Beyond Belief

Downtrodden

They were afraid of the witches,
When it was their beliefs that were unclean,
They didn't really know God,
Whose words were still unseen.

Misunderstanding became a ruler,
Of a very nefarious sort,
The wretched inquisition,
And what their fear would so distort.

So many false accusations,
No enemies of God,
The war crimes of religion,
But upon truth it cannot trod.

Beyond Belief

Metaphoric Light

Collective Coup

There are beliefs I don't buy into,
Fads designed to distract,
No thank you, I am more interested in,
Taking my sovereign power back.

Maybe it's not about fitting in,
To illusionary things,
Maybe it's about finding my own truth,
And listening to how it sings.

To step out of the confusion,
To cut programming's ties,
To disconnect from fuckery,
To banish all the lies.

To disentangle from the falsehoods,
Which might contaminate my space,
To recognize my divinity,
Which flows out now from grace.

It doesn't stem from any belief system,
Which functions through ego feed,
And it really isn't necessary,
To sit and let it bleed.

To say no to the inappropriate,
Where peer pressure does not rule,
To overlay with wisdom,
That which misleads the fool.

To say no to the brimstone and hellfire,
Sold from a pompous stage,
To call my energy back,
From any wayward rage.

I recognize the corruption,
Which tries to overtake the earth,
I choose not to engage in it,
I am here for my rebirth.

Spirit Silver Moon

Metaphoric Light

Orchestrations

Old weapons no longer deadly,
In the fields where memories burn,
New choices create new experiences,
Orchestrated by what we learn.

Strength gained through tribulation,
Seeing beyond illusion's dream,
To the power in the laughter,
Which eventually follows the scream.

No victims beyond the temporary,
New vision through metaphoric eyes,
No tangled power over us, ever,
From the valley of terrible lies.

When greed no longer feeds the flames,
But sits as a mound of ash,
When control and fear and jealousy,
Don't trigger ego to attack.

When compassion bursts forth like a shining light,
The light which leads us home,
Then and only then,
Have we managed to atone.

Janine Palmer (Silver Moon)

Her layers are deep,
Her bubble gum walls,
The myth and the mystery,
Keeps her enthralled.

Metaphoric Light

When Ambience Speaks

She takes places of loneliness and makes
them inviting. She invites them to tell stories.
Still life as art.

Metaphoric Light

An open window,
To fresher air,
As whispers fly,
From sacred lairs.

Those who listen,
To higher self,
To disengage,
From illusion's hell.

Metaphoric Light

Something more gracious,
For the seeker awaits,
As we move back to love,
Not prisoners of hate.

Metaphoric Light

A dragon's lair,
Where treasure's kept,
And what was cleared,
From when she wept.

To let it flow,
For it must move,
And there are truths,
We don't need to prove.

Metaphoric Light

Perspectives

Those stuck in rigid patriarchal programming
might feel uncomfortable in the loving and
powerful energy of the goddess.

Perspectives

People show up for us in different ways and
in different roles in different lifetimes, for
what we need to learn and heal.

Perspectives

You shouldn't have to hide your emotions,
Especially if pushed too far,
You don't need to be ashamed of what you feel,
You're beautiful as you are.

Perspectives

In tune with truth,
Not learned on earth,
A glorious spark,
Of our rebirth.

A recognition,
Or a disconnect,
To re-instate,
Our self-respect.

Perspectives

Boundaries of thorns,
Or boundaries of light,
Something more truthful,
Within us burns bright.

Perspectives

Sword fights for honor,
Or hired blades,
Fighting true or false battles,
False enemies made.

Perspectives

Some no longer serve the church,
They choose only to serve God,
And the pathways back home heavenward,
Are many which we all trod.

Perspectives

Charting courses through unknown territory,
For experience and treasure to be gained,
Wisdom extracted and emotions processed,
As truth and balance are maintained.

Perspectives

About the Author

Janine Palmer (Silver Moon) is a writer of esoteric and energy healing messages. She writes from her own healing experiences and observations which lead to deeper wisdom.

She is a Clinical Hypnotherapist and Shamanic Practitioner who is passionate about emotional and spiritual healing.

She speaks of sacred truth, hidden keys, and light and shadow. She reminds us to remember, honor and embrace our divine worthiness and to step out of programming.

She shines light on the power of forgiveness and the beauty we hold within. Her work might be helpful or of interest to those working through the initiations of spiritual alchemy and realigning to the love we always are, our innate truth.

~ The loving energy is evident – MG

~ **Your poetry is like humanity singing for things that most of us can't put into words – SS**

~ Beautiful – AS

~ A'ho – UL

~ **I'm sure enjoying your book. I love it. Your wisdom my dear, and your remembrance of soul from ages past. It just brings it back. It's beautiful, Janine, it really is. I just appreciate it so much – AA**

~ Love this - CH

~ Wow, a lovely piece of truth and honesty and hope to move forward – SD

~ **I love what you write – AF**

~ It really is beautiful. You're very talented my dear. You put these things into words that resonate. Really valuable. Really worth a lot to me - AWA

~ New gates indeed. Wonderfully penned by dear friend – JM

~ Very good – DS

~ Bravo Sistar – TSP

~ Beautiful – DR

~ Truly said, when we are through learning we are through – SW

~ **This is epic Janine Palmer, total truth and LOVE is the answer – DS**

~ Beautiful and Sharing – MB

~ **I'm one of your biggest fans. You and your beautiful poetry has helped me so much on my journey. I know you and your gift will help many others navigate their journey. I will always share and support you. So much love to you Sister – TSP**

~ Well penned – JM

~ You are so uplifting – TMM

~ Lovely words – SD

~ Love this beautiful Sister poet!!! – CH

~ Nice post. Thanks for taking the time to write it – MK

~ Arise and be known – JM

~ Incredible – MB

~ **I'm already halfway through 'Love Notes to Self'. Thank you so much. I believe that your words are what I needed most in my life right now... Love you sister! – KS**

~ Well stated – JM

~ People fear your wisdom 'honestly' truth because you're a messenger from the highest order and people fear your light. The light of humanity that wipes away the darkness and shows us our divine presence and glory to serve but one true God. And serve it you must – SD

~ Love this – JM

~ Love this Janine Palmer – CH

~ **I love what you do. Your writing is very healing - WG**

~ Love that. After reading your work, I find myself in a fantastic fantasy at times. Even inspired to write my own. Just know I support you and your work – JM

~ **Love everything written here – SD**

~ Thank you – GL

~ Ever grateful for YOU Beautiful Sister Poet of Wisdom and Enlightenment!!!!!! Big loves and brightest of Blessings always! - CH

~ **Totally agree!!! Absolutely love this content Janine – SD**

~ The Wisdom of Mysteries…. – SJ

~ For my English friends, only words of wisdom – AV

~ Beautiful – NFW

~ Thank you, Janine Palmer – TM

~ Truth – DR

~ Love This, Beautiful You – TSP

~ Brilliant – JA

~ Awesome! – DR

~ **What I love so much is this Ink dear Sister!!! And You!!! A very Sacred Healing piece! Ever grateful beautiful heart! – CH**

~ Love this – DN

~ Gorgeous! Simply, Deeply, Gorgeous – HR

~ Very, very good, Janine Palmer! – DS

~ Thank you – CH

~ AMEN – NFW

~ **Perfect timing! – AH**

~ AWESOME – AC

~ Yes. True – NFW

~ Sharing! – FD

~ Yasss…this is right on target - FD

~ Awesome – UL

~ Ahhh I love this beautiful. Thank you – CH

~ Those last 4 lines are heavy. Soulful indeed – SW

~ Thank you, I love you – CS

~ Amen – PR

~ **Absolutely precious – BLS**

~ Love this – CD

~ **Absolutely beautiful words – JB**

~ Beautiful – BD

~ Yess!!! Onto the next adventure – AB
~ Love this! – AS
~ Luv – SN
~ You are a gift to humanity. Words unspoken but understood. That is your gift xoxo – SG
~ Love it Beautiful! – AS
~ Completely different aesthetic… - BP
~ **Beautiful as well as heartfelt – FT**
~ Thank you for this beautiful poem – UL
~ Beautiful – MB
~ SO LOVE THIS – MS
~ Deep bow and heartfelt thank YOU Beautiful Muse and Sister!!! Ever grateful for the Magick you share with us – CH
~ You've got a real gift of capturing some beautiful ideas and setting forth others – MK
~ Amen – LH
~ The eloquence of your beautiful words seduces my soul and evokes the passionate side which was dormant and uninspired for too long! More in adoration and awe I could not be! Your very essence is pure poetry to me! – EV
~ Thank you, Janine, – CH
~ Janine Palmer's shit is FIRE!!!! Love it! - DS
~ I love this sis, Bravo Beautiful You – TSP

~ Definitely a little bit of me in here – SD

~ Amazing Ink Sister!! – CH

~ **I must agree undeniably – JT**

~ Love the words and that inviting fire Janine – SD

~ Love this! – DS

~ **Absolutely beautiful. I love your imagery and the hope you offer in the dark – MW**

~ Did you know that you have connections with angels? Every time I see you picture you are glowing – MCM

~ **Gorgeous! Simply, Deeply Gorgeous – HR**

~ Very, very good Janine Palmer! – DS

~ Love this – DN

~ Thank you, Janine Palmer, – CH

~ What I love so much about this ink dear Sister and you...it's a very Sacred, Healing piece! Every grateful beautiful heart! – CH

~ It's strange but I can feel your soul, what you write, your wisdom – AF

~ **Very Good, thou wordsmithy – MG**

~ My God you have found the meaning of the image of the photo. Beautiful words that have the truth. You have a great gift of interpreting images or photos. I'm speechless. This poem of your will be framed on the wall of my

house. Thank you, you made a masterpiece –
AF

~ I want you to know this is probably in my top 10 favorite posts of all time. It's loaded with truth. Thank you! – AH

~ Just beautiful – SD